Gold In The Rough

An assortment of delectable poems

Catherine Halim

BookLeaf
Publishing

India | USA | UK

Dedication

This collection of poems is dedicated to every single brain and heart I've encountered along the way. The person I am today would not exist without the impact of your one-of-a-kind presence in my life.

Preface

Gold in the Rough is a collection of poems that have
been birthed, gathered and refined during a pivotal
season of my life. It was a time when I faced a cancer
diagnosis and had to navigate the hard and fast idea that
the new year would look significantly (and I mean
significantly) different to the years prior. Despite the
"devastation" and "destruction" a cancer diagnosis is
usually tied to, I decided to see my personal experience
of cancer as a once-in-a-lifetime opportunity and
nothing short of a blessing in disguise and a breeding
ground for joy.

As an English teacher by trade, I have carefully curated
and structured some poems in a particular way, to
provide readers & (my students) with a catalyst for their
own creative expressions and storytelling. The poems
within this collection touch on and explore the
intricacies of identity, the steadfast beauty of faith, and
the vulnerability of life.

The poems have been broken up into three sections:
i. prelude - pre op./pre treat.
ii. the in-between - resting on the foundation of faith
iii. legacy - to self, to others, to you

The Creator's Guide 🎨

✏️ - first line starter

⚒️ - use the skeletal structure of the poem to customise

✧ - add EXTRA details to personalise

i. prelude - pre op./pre treat.

An echo of myself #200 ✧

A surge of Amnesia #217

ALIVE ✏️ ⚒️

Traces of you are in me

dawns on me #252 ✏️

The river won't run dry #254 ✧

ii. the in-between - resting on the foundation of faith

Grounded #212 ⚒️

Slowing to Solitude #231

Sovereign #232

Peace #255

Comfort #256 ✏️ ⚒️

Joy #257

iii. legacy - to self, to others, to you

dear future me,

gifted to my daughter

every chance as you #251

just 15

knowing someone #250

stripped raw #253

to mama

to papa

to you

Acknowledgements

First and foremost, I would not be here today without my God, who has been a constant source and carrier of peace, comfort, and joy. I'd also like to acknowledge the enormous support I've received from my cherished family (thank you TJ), wise mentors and coaches, and my hardcore, handpicked wildflowers in a luscious green field sorta friends.

A special thank you to my gold standard brother, Tim, who designed the front cover.

It was really in the quiet and still moments, though – sometimes at really inconvenient times – that creativity sparked and a poem was formed.

An echo of myself

I write...
Bits of poetry...
Bits of music...
Bits of who I am down on a page...
Leaving behind my legacy for the reader to find
My innermost thoughts and feelings and all that
I know of as true.

What do you write?
What do you listen to?
I bite my lip as I conceal the fact that I don't like to show
these parts of me to the world...cause the arrangement of
words entwined with melody and all sorts that resonate
with me spells out 3 words, 13 letters... I am vulnerable.

But the lines of poetry and the notes of music,
they hold much more,
they carry hidden weight,
they are an echo of my soul...
raw and vivid, private and intimate.

And sometimes, just sometimes I do like to keep
this part of me
hidden — an echo of myself

A surge of Amnesia

we have these moments in life
that seem to slip from our memory,
simply escaping the tight grasp of remembering,
and, when we do regain consciousness,
we tell ourselves over and over:
I will not forget,
    I won't forget,
        i won't,
            i forget;
that's where we slip over the edge
back into the ebbing flow of the sea of amnesia
erratic yet fluid, coming in tides
and right before we are entirely submerged, skin
engulfed in its flow
lungs   desperate,
gasping,
for
the
taste of
air   .
Our hearts reacquaints, reconnects, reunites with the
part of the brain
where we remember - who we are,
what it is like to know completely,

without a flicker of a doubt,
as one makes note of what to know for next time
when a surge of amnesia strikes again:

#217

ALIVE

I feel...

alone

the kind where you're sitting in a row of your own with
a room full of people,
the kind where you're standing in the middle of the field
with the lights off and the rain pouring down until
you're completely, utterly soaked, head-to-toe drenched
the kind where you're in the bathroom stall where
you've had to get yourself into a space of your own
just so you can stop.
and stand.
and focus again on how to

B...ball up your fists
R..relax your shoulders
E...exhale long
A...allow your lungs to fill again
T...teach your fingers to relax and release
H...hear the sound of your exhale
E...

i've thought about sleeping deep and
of running into the forest and staying lost
(you know disappearing off the grid, untraceable, just
out of touch)
of driving not knowing where we are heading or when
and if

i say i'm fine
i say i'll live
i say were good

and I stop cause I realise I'm not, I'm not done yet.

I simply just feel...

A L I V E

Traces of You are in Me

The first time I laid eyes on you was
when I saw the lines
in my oaky brown wooden floorboards
and
the time I stared out the window
and again
In the veins hidden behind my smooth almond wrists
You were always meant to be a part of me
.

A piece is laid down
A shattered broken glass
A fragmented shard that on it's own is on it's way
ready to be discarded
But as I wait...
patiently
another piece is laid down before me
Just another fractured jagged piece of glass

And as moments go by
piece after piece is laid down
And behold,
Now what's before us
starts to soon take shape and form
And as I raise my head, I see her giving me

the last piece she has of herself
And as she lets go of her will to cling on
I take hold of the missing piece she so dearly defended
all this time

And alas a mirror is formed, standing before us,
shattered pieces fit to form one

***

That's where it clicked for me,
Knowing that we are just the same broken pieces,
Shattered unapologetically alone,
But when assembled together
We become a reflection
of the very one standing before us.

The same fragilities
The same vulnerabilities
The same smudged glimmers on the mirrored glass
Yet one image before me
Yet one resounding voice
Whispering, echoing: you are a part of me.

dawns on me

it dawns on me that
we are mortal
that death could occur
but that
it could occur to anyone really

the chances of me living
is something
similar to the probability
of someone else
i just may have a clue as to what
"the cause of death" could be
but still
it's still a "could,"
a probability,
some statistical data,
someone out there may try and make sense of

even when we take a look at life
we learn that
life does not always
stick to the path we map it out to be
who cares what the "facts" state anyways

so we think we got a real chance?
well we can't completely control the outcome anyways
what we can do though is:
we can steer it towards a particular destination of course
but really
the WHO, the HOW, the WHY may stay a mystery
we can just control the present
and what we choose to do with the present
while we are alive

so what dawns on me exactly?
how i'll choose to live until
there's no more choosing
and it dawns on me with arms open wide

#252

the river won't run dry

i get this image of a river
a river that flows down
i often think i should keep this river hidden,
a place of my own,
no one needs to see it, hear it, feel it,
thinking it'll run dry if the world were to know,
but what if...

and as i slowly remove the foliage that has kept it
so securely hidden,
and let those that stumble upon it
stay for as long as they please,
I realise, they can experience what the river can bring
a refreshment of sorts,
for some it even provides them with healing,
and others the sounds of the waters stirs up comfort, as
the waters flow down, gush down against the rocks far
down below

though the waters rise higher than some days,
and lower on others,
I realise this: that the river won't run dry

#254

GROUNDED.

Something about laying on the cold hard floor at night
grounds me.
Reminds me that I am just dirt,
Nothing morbid but there's something comforting about
knowing that you've got a creator in your midst and that
you are dirt, his dirt.
Easily moulded and shaped into anything you want
yourself to be.
And everything around you is forced to slow down.

Something about laying on the cold hard floor at night
makes me grateful.
Often if I lay there for more than a minute I get in a
naturally nostalgic mood reminiscing about my life,
the what and the who
And where I'll be

Something about laying on the cold hard floor at night
activates my heart and mind
Setting it into perfect harmony.
That without one there is no other.
No hierarchy, just levelled synchrony.
My heart slows it's beating and my mind clears
leaving room for my heart to speak its mind.

Something about laying on the cold hard floor at night
looking up and seeing the world from a different angle.
Different from the other 17 hours of the day. Knowing
that the lens I use to see through, may not be the only
lens I carry.

#212

Slowing to Solitude

cause we need to remind ourselves
to slow down before the crash,
to slow down and take in His faithfulness,
to slow down and be grateful a little more.

cause with each and every day we choose to neglect
what our insides are saying, we let the void,
meant for Him to be filled with something else,
when it really should be space
sacred
left for Him alone
selah,

so remind me once again, to slow down when I need to,
to slow down and listen to my heart's yearning for a
place of solitude with you.

#231

Sovereign

I am not in the mood to cry - I used to say to myself

Yet I know the pain I carry is boiling over whatever container I am trying to force close just to inhibit the growth of what is growing, festering, flourishing? inside.

Because if I am able to contain them, restrict them, govern over them, I am able to withhold my most raw parts of me from crumbling all over the place, leaving scattered shattered smithereens wherever the footsteps of this heart trails.

I've learnt that I often go into a "do not feel" state, because somewhere along the way I was taught:
1. to feel is to be weak,
2. those feelings are not valid,
3. darling, why do you feel?
So to survive I suppress, I numb and in the process, I hold the agonising sting of pain, until I forget and no longer feel, until that one fleeting moment, where yes it slips, I slip, I merely forget that I have so tightly imprisoned my feelings held captive in my heart where days, turn to weeks and weeks turn into months and into

years infiltrating into seasons...of solitary confinement,
I need,
NO MUST keep my hands clenched down on it so it does
NOT spill ov-
er,
but sometimes, sometimes
I leave it unguarded and it goes gushing out,
unrestrained. Almost uncontrollable. Almost makes me
feel unrecognisable. Almost as if they are not mine, yet it
is undeniable.

One can not hold this, this myriad of "I feel" alone, but
all I want to do when these emotions arise is to be alone,
cause when I let silence take over that is when I am able
to feel, that is when I am able to be myself, for myself
and with myself.

And then it grasps me,
the resounding words,
speak,
"Then Jesus wept."
Wept because something had been lost, no not Lazarus,
but in the people...I had often been blinded and we have
missed something that when these waves of "so called
feelings" wash me over completely I let it now cause it
reminds me that I am only human and He is God,
sovereign over all.

I am hurting,
But I am also healing,
Cause the path to healing is back through my hurt,
back through my pain that I
refused
to feel years ago...until I heal
and know, with all that I am, that He is sovereign over
ALL.

#232

peace

peace runs deep in my veins,
a stillness
a calmness
that does not shake

Have I always had this peace? I ponder to myself.
the answer - *no*
that although,
the peace in me:
feels formidable, unrelenting, unwavering
it was not always there

the first I had felt it was when I was in ruins,
young, naive, broken
are we not all _______ in some shape and form?
where chaos felt like the only compass
I could yield my hands on
and it was only then,
that one dark, lonely night, as I sat on the cold hard floor,
or was it
that one warm sunny afternoon as I sat on my bed,
a guitar in hand
that I had realised it didn't have to be this way.

and I gave up the need to feel in control of my emotions.
I decided instead to let go and surrender to the potential
that God could hear me,
that He could hear my cry,
and
He enveloped me right there and then
with peace that has never left me.

#255

comfort

comfort is an interesting thing
it reminds me of adding sugar in freshly brewed
English Breakfast Tea
or
licking the froth off a sweet milk hot chocolate

comfort is an interesting thing
it is a soft to touch, smell of fresh linen fabric softener
wafting into one's lungs, deep and full, as a fluffy blanket
lays atop goose-bumped skin
or
the touch of soft baked sand that simply falls off
the balls of our fingertips

comfort is an interesting thing
it sounds like two friends deep in conversation as they
share stories about life as they know it
or
the sound of shared space, where silence is nothing short
of comfort-able and satiating stillness

#256

joy

joy doesn't have to mimic what others find happiness in,
it is it's own form of pure contentment, electric ecstasy,
it's a state of mind and perspective my mentors say,
it's the spirit you bring,
the way you carry yourself,
the way you choose to see,
the way you choose to be
in your own right, joy cannot be taken away from you
because joy, always, has been a choice for the taking.

#257

dear future me,

when you see a mountain in the distance,
invite growing excitement to stir deep inside,
knowing that when a mountain presents itself,
it's yet another chance for you to see yourself and
your creator in a new light,

knowing that the struggle up the mountain is where
you'll grow the most
and
after conquering the hardest part of the climb,
know with the deepest essence of who you are that:
you will reach the top,
as you always do,
stronger, fitter, better
with graced humility singed with bold fierceness
knowing
that there lies ahead
is yet another mountain calling for you to conquer and
be victorious over.

and when you do glance back,
just for a moment,
be kind to mountains you've climbed and conquered.
They were just moulding you up for who you are to be.

dear future me
the mountain is you
and every single version of who you used to be

#239

gifted to my daughter

When I should have a daughter
I'd tell her to not shy away from falling over, to fall if she must, and do it with a "I'm getting back up, just you watch" smile on her face,
I'd tell her to yell back when 'required' of course and to face boys head on, with fire in her eyes, and her heart on her sleeve, knowing that she can yank her heart back whole if she needs to

When I should have a daughter I'd tell her to stand on her very own two feet,
To know that she could outrun anyone that's up for a challenge and to never back down.

When I should have a daughter I'd show her to think outside of the box, wait no, there is no box except for what SHE thinks she is capable of (and no one has a right to box her in like that).

When I should have a daughter I'd show her how to be her own role model,
To be the voice for the voiceless,
To understand the misunderstood, and
To fight (with very few punches possible) for those

that have very little fight left in them.

When I should have a daughter I want her to know that
she's her own person,
that she is whole and worthy and enough, always,
always enough,
despite how she may feel right at this moment.

When I should have a daughter,
I'd show her what it means to fly, to soar, solo if needed,
yet knowing if she must fly solo
that she is never truly alone.

When I should have a daughter,
I'll call her my own,
and she will know that she is loved beyond anything that
she could ever do to earn it
cause love is:
unconditional, unwavering, unending.

When I should have a daughter I'd tell her much more
than this, but for now THIS will be it.

every chance as you

cancer has caused me to realise that
I have every chance of dying as you
I might just know the cause of death
dying is in the cards for me, as it is for you
sooo really who's in the win?
at least I've got a chance to reflect on death before it
happens, "we all are mortal after all,"
so it'll happen to all of us - the passing?

I have every chance of living as you
I might just know how I want to live and
the cause for living
living is in the cards for me, as it is for you
sooo really who's in the loss?
at most I've got a chance to reflect on life before I don't
get the chance to.

we have every chance of living...and dying,
whether we are consciously aware of it or not
we all get given a hand,
a stack of cards that must be dealt
sooo really what are the chances?

#251

just 15

when my daughter turns 15
imma tell her this:
that life is hard,
but so are diamonds,
and baby girl,
you are a diamond waiting to happen,
diamond in the rough,
being grinded and formed into shape,
so honey pot (i think I like that name),
honey pot, just you watch,
you'll glisten from every angle,
and I mean every angle.

life is gonna suck so bad sometimes,
and you'll remember what your mama told you,
get **grounded**, lay on the cold hard floor and let your
heart and mind synchronise
until YOU remember who YOU are and who YOU plan
on becoming, cause look how far you've come to be
where you are in this very moment.

so remember this: give yourself time, give yourself grace,
give yourself the chance to just be 15.

knowing someone

we say we never really
learn who someone is until...
one's health is on the line,
until they say we found something coincidentally,
until they say they are mildly suspicious,
until they say they could be cancerous,
until they say, "are you okay?"
until they pause, silence, "i don't want to overload you
but..."

a phone call ended. months passed. a nap has passed.

until your left side feels funny
until a headache
until vision get blurred,
until you don't believe it could be a pinched nerve,
until you request an MRI to be done,
spine, along with the brain

your first set of testing was done

until they call you in and say come back
when we are closed,
until they sit you down and say, "unfortunately we found

a tumour and unfortunately it's not benign"
until, they say i called and they just had a cancellation,
until they say i'm not sure about him, but if you're not
happy we can get a second opinion,
until they say they think its a low grade 2 or 3,

a late night gym session was done - cause you're not sure
if it could be the last...

until they call you and say, "the team would like you to
do another set of testing,"
until they say, it's more aggressive than we thought
until they say and now its a possible grade 3, low grade 4
until they say, so we want to get it out, unless
you want to give it some more time to process

processed.

let's get it done.
until he says, "can you speak to all my other patients"
until you become a patient
until you get discharged from ICU, along with the
hospital a few days later
until pathology gets back to proff.
until it's confirmed that it was grade 3 and
the area around the tumour already had cancer cells
and I guess that's when

stripped raw

that it is not all about
surviving
or
about getting a good prognosis, diagnosis, whatever-osis
or
not hearing bad or good news
or
not relapsing or being completely healed

it's about even if...
can you keep being authentically you?
can you still be compassionate and kind, even if you've
been dealt a tough hand?
can you keep living in a way that makes people feel
seen, heard and felt?
can you keep being the version of you, the version that
you've willed and called yourself to be, despite
"everything" that has been stripped from you?
can you be stripped raw and still be you?

if you were to be stripped raw to the core?
what would you find? who would you find?

#253

to mama

now I know what it means to be cared for twice over
to have you there for every waking moment
the times I wiggled and laid there unable to sleep

a list of thank yous:
for doing laps around the house with me,
as I steadied my feet once again and
taught my body how to recall a sense of balance,
for cooking up every cuisine from
ayam kiamboi to lamb cutlets
to garlic shrimp pasta
to Jen's banana cake with a dash of rum (of course),
for taking me to the gym as I reclaimed
the strength and agility I had
and even took it up a notch,
for sharing some of my temporary hobbies
of lego building, colouring and fitness,
that I even got you to jog a little,

I have realised the prayers, the yapping and the humour,
started with you and now it runs deep in me

so for that: thank you for believing that miracles can
continue to happen.

to papa

now,
that i'm much older
I know what it means
to take shelter under the wings of a father,
my heavenly and my earthly father,
a double dosing,
a roof on top of my head,
a bed of my choice to rest on,
food at the table,
"its yours" you say, "you don't need to ask"
my double dosing of abba father blessings

to you

[to Tim and Jane]
siblings I thank God for over and over,
a gift of two,
the yin and yang in my eyes,
like having two armed soldiers, one on each side,
an addition I started with, and now I have another,
I get to have two!

[to the unexpected friendship]
the blessing:
to spar with and get sharp with,
to pray and be prayed for with,
to brighten the torch I have in hand and
to line up my fiery arrows with.
What a joy it has been, to be known as your friend.

[to my amigos]
"slap that on the list"
yes, yes and yes again.
who knew some friendships would be forged in this way,
accelerated in "the darkest of nights,"
but this friendship right here is
like the rise of a fresh morning over the
sparkle-lit waters of daylight

[to the MCs of Cat's brain and heart]
You've bloomed and blossomed,
Your colours rarely just few,
Right when you needed to, with timing anew.
At the right place and the right time,
you came like dawn,
And although seasons will change,
and petals will be gone,
There was beauty in every stage,
a beauty to call you on..

[to my reader]
I leave you with this,
gold in the rough,
to know that even in the toughest seasons,
when trials are rough,
you are gold, distinct and have always,
always been enough.